Lives of the Saints

Saint Francis
with Prayers and Devotions

Edited by
Mark Etling

Nihil Obstat:	Reverend Robert O. Morrissey, J.C.D. Censor librorum March 24, 2003
Imprimatur:	Most Reverend William Murphy Bishop of Rockville Centre March 31, 2003

THE REGINA PRESS
10 Hub Drive
Melville, New York 11747
www.reginapress.com

All rights reserved. No part of this publication may be reproduced or transmitted in any form or by any means, electronic or mechanical, including photocopying, recording, or any information storage and retrieval system, without permission in writing from the publishers.

© Copyright 2003, 2007 by The Regina Press.

Florentine Collection™, All rights reserved worldwide.
Imported exclusively by Malco.

Printed in U.S.A.

ISBN: 9780882717432

Introduction

*F*rancis of Assisi is certainly one of the most universally known and loved of all the saints. Christians and non-Christians alike are inspired and edified by his life. It is not hard to understand why this is so. Francis bears witness to the belief that the straightest path to God is the path of our deepest humanity.

St. Francis was passionately devoted to God, and his every action was motivated by his love for God. He adopted a radically simple lifestyle because he placed his trust in God, and not in his possessions. He was compassionate to those who were poor or sick because he believed every man and woman was his brother or sister. His love of nature and for all of God's creatures was easy for him because he understood everything was created by God, and thus everything is good. Francis was a humble man because he believed every action of his was performed not to bring glory to himself, but to God.

In short, it is his humanity that makes Francis of Assisi a holy person - a saint. He never ran away from and never denied his humanity.

Rather, he embraced it, loved it, lived it fully - and in so doing, found the road to sanctity and union with God.

This book about St. Francis is written in that spirit. As we reflect on his life and as we pray for his intercession, we should remember that Francis is a saint precisely because he is so human.

The Life of St. Francis

How strange the behavior of their son Francis must have seemed to his father and mother, Piero and Pica Bernardone.

For the first twenty years of his life, young Francis had lived a normal and fairly uneventful life. Born in the Italian village of Assisi in 1182, he had worked in the family business with Piero, a wealthy cloth merchant. In 1202, he had fought on the side of Assisi in a war against the neighboring province of Perugia, and had been taken prisoner for several months.

After returning home from his imprisonment, Francis' life began to change in ways his parents could not comprehend. He suffered a severe illness, during which he became dissatisfied with his worldly lifestyle. He resolved to change his life and to devote himself to prayer and service of the poor.

On a pilgrimage to Rome, Francis was moved by compassion for the beggars who gathered in front of St. Peter's Basilica. He exchanged his clothes with one of the beggars and spent a day begging for alms.

After returning to Assisi, Francis began to

minister to lepers and to rebuild churches that had fallen into disrepair. He even sold a bale of silk from his father's warehouse to pay for the church repairs. This angered Piero Bernardone so much that he disowned Francis. Yet his son did not back down. He laid his clothing at the feet of his father and walked away naked. He declared himself wedded to "Lady Poverty," renounced all of his worldly possessions and devoted himself completely to serving the poor.

Francis continued his work of rebuilding churches and ministering to lepers. In 1206 he heard the voice of Christ: "Francis, go out and build up my house, for it is nearly falling down." He understood this as a call to rebuild the church at San Damiano, a task he gladly and immediately took on. He went begging door to door, scrounging for discarded bread and vegetables from the trash when he could not get money for his repair work on the church. He asked to be paid for his work in bread, milk, eggs, or vegetables rather than money.

He also devoted his time to caring for lepers in the woods near Mt. Subiaco. At that time, lepers were kept at a distance and regarded with fear and disgust. Francis' attitude was entirely different. He cared for the lepers by bathing them, feeding them and kissing them.

In 1208 Francis began to preach the Gospel after receiving his call from God at Portiuncula, a village near Assisi. He gathered twelve disciples around him who became known for the long dark garments they wore girded with a cord, and for traveling about without staff and shoes. They elected Francis superior, and he wrote a simple Rule for them based on sayings from the Gospels.

Pope Innocent III formally recognized Francis and his followers in 1210, by authorizing the formation of the Franciscans, officially known as the Order of Friars Minor. ("Friar" is derived from the word "brother," and the Franciscans considered themselves "brothers in Christ"). The brothers would have no money and no property, either individually or collectively. Their calling was to preach, declaring by their words and their actions the love of Christ.

The small band of Franciscan friars settled in huts at Rivoreto and Portiuncula. They traveled throughout central Italy, preaching for people to turn from the world to Christ. Francis and his followers emphasized poverty and simplicity, relying on God's providence rather than worldly possessions. The brothers worked or begged for what they needed, and the surplus was given to the poor.

In 1212, Francis received Clara Sciffi, a girl from a noble family, into their fellowship. With his help she established the Order of Poor Ladies, also knows as the Poor Clares, at San Damiano.

Over time, Francis became renowned for his love of all God's creatures. A story is told about a wolf who was terrorizing the people of Gubbio, a village north of Assisi. Francis learned that the wolf was killing and eating both animals and people. Francis decided to go out and meet the wolf, believing God would take care of him.

One friar and several villagers went out with him, but before long the villagers turned back in fear. Suddenly the wolf came out of the woods and confronted Francis and the friar. Francis made the Sign of the Cross at the wolf, and the animal slowed down and closed its mouth. Then Francis called out to the animal: "Come to me, Brother Wolf. In the name of Christ I order you not to hurt anyone." The wolf lowered his head and lay down at Francis' feet.

Francis again addressed the wolf: "Brother Wolf, I want to make peace between you and the people of Gubbio. They will harm you no more and you must no longer harm them. All past crimes are to be forgiven." The wolf moved its body and nodded its head in agreement.

Then Francis ordered the wolf to follow him into town and make peace with the villagers. The wolf meekly followed Francis. When they arrived at the town square, Francis asked for a pledge of peace between the villagers and the wolf, and all agreed. The wolf lived for two years among the villagers, going door to door for food. When the wolf died of old age, the villagers of Gubbio mourned his passing.

In 1214, Francis felt called to preach the Good News of Christ to the Moors, Muslim people who lived in Spain and north Africa. He made his way through the south of France and into Spain, but illness prevented him from reaching Africa.

In 1219, Francis journeyed with eleven of his companions to eastern Europe and Egypt during the Fifth Crusade. He preached among the Muslims, and tried to convert their sultan, Melek-al-Kamil. As a demonstration of his faith,

Francis proposed to the sultan that a fire be built, and that he and a Muslim volunteer walk side by side into the fire to show whose faith was stronger. The sultan said he was not sure a volunteer could be found. Francis then volunteered to walk into the fire alone. Even though the sultan was deeply impressed, he remained unconverted. Francis then traveled on to the Holy Land, and as a result of the trip, the Franciscans were given custody of the Christian shrines there that had been under Muslim control for centuries.

On his return from the Holy Land in 1220, Francis learned of dissension among the friars and resigned as superior. The following year, he agreed to a new modified Rule called the *Regula Prima*, and he spent the next few years planning the Tertiaries, or the Third Order of Franciscans.

In the early fall of 1224, Francis made a retreat on Mt. Alverna in the Apennine Mountains. There, after a forty-day fast, he received the Stigmata, the reproduction of the wounds of Christ, in his own body.

The last few years of Francis' life were marked by pain and suffering, and almost total blindness. On his deathbed, he repeated over and over the last addition to his *Canticle to the Sun*: "Be praised, O Lord, for our Sister Death."

Francis of Assisi died in the chapel of Portiuncula at the age of 44 on October 3, 1226. Because his holiness and the depth of his devotion to God were so well known, he was canonized in 1228, just two years after his death.

Prayers of St. Francis

St. Francis of Assisi's Vocation Prayer

Most High, glorious God,
   enlighten the darkness of our minds.
Give us a right faith, a firm hope and a perfect charity,
   so that we may always and in all things act according to your holy will.
   Amen.

*The Meditation Prayer of
St. Francis of Assisi*

My God and my all!

St. Francis' Prayer Before the Crucifix

Most High, glorious God,
   enlighten the darkness of my heart and give me true faith, certain hope,
   and perfect charity,
sense and knowledge, Lord,

that I may carry out
your holy and true command. Amen

St. Francis of Assisi's Prayer in Praise of God Given to Brother Leo

You are holy, Lord, the only God,
  and Your deeds are wonderful.
You are strong.
You are great.
You are the Most High.
You are Almighty.
You, Holy Father, are King of heaven and earth.
You are Three and One, Lord God, all good.
You are good, all good, supreme good,
Lord God, living and true.
You are love. You are wisdom.
You are humility. You are endurance.
You are rest. You are peace.
You are joy and gladness.
You are justice and moderation.
You are all our riches, and you suffice for us.
You are beauty.
You are gentleness.
You are our protector.
You are our guardian and defender.

You are our courage.
You are our haven and our hope.
You are our faith, our great consolation.
You are our eternal life, great and
  wonderful Lord,
God almighty, merciful Savior

The Blessing of St. Francis of Assisi to Brother Leo

The Lord bless you and keep you.
May he show his face to you and
  have mercy.
May he turn his countenance to you
  and give you peace.
The Lord bless you!

Prayer of St. Francis of Assisi Before the Blessed Sacrament

We adore you, O Lord Jesus Christ,
  in this church and all the churches
  of the world, and we bless you because,
  by your holy Cross you have redeemed
the world.

Canticle of Brother Sun and Sister Moon to St. Francis of Assisi

Most High, all-powerful, all-good Lord,
All praise is yours, all glory,
   all honor and all blessings.
To you alone, Most High, do they belong,
   and no mortal lips are worthy to
pronounce your name.

Praised be you my Lord
   and with all your creatures,
   especially Sir Brother Sun,
Who is the day through whom you
   give us light.
And he is beautiful and radiant with
   great splendor,
Of you Most High, he bears the likeness.

Praised be you, my Lord, through Sister
Moon and the stars,
In the heavens you have made them bright,
precious and fair.

Praised be you, my Lord, through Brothers
Wind and Air,

And fair and stormy, all weather's moods,
by which you cherish all that you have made.
Praised be you my Lord through
   Sister Water,
So useful, humble, precious and pure.

Praised be you my Lord through
   Brother Fire,
   through whom you light the night
   and he is beautiful and playful and robust
      and strong.

Praised be you my Lord through our sister,
Mother Earth who sustains and governs us,
producing varied fruits with colored flowers
   and herbs.
Praised be you my Lord through those who
grant pardon for love of you
   and bear sickness and trial.
Blessed are those who endure in peace,
By you Most High, they will be crowned.

Praised be you, my Lord through Sister Death,
   from whom no-one living can escape.
Woe to those who die in mortal sin!
Blessed are they she finds doing your will.

No second death can do them harm.
Praise and bless my Lord and give him thanks,
And serve him with great humility.

St. Francis of Assisi's Prayer Praising Mary the Mother of Jesus

Hail, holy lady, most holy queen,
Mary, Mother of God, ever virgin.
You were chosen by the
Most High Father in heaven,
   consecrated by him, with his most holy beloved Son
   and the Holy Spirit, the Comforter.

On you descended and still remains all the fullness of grace and every good.
Hail his palace. Hail his tabernacle.
Hail his robe. Hail his handmaid.
Hail his Mother.
And hail, all holy virtues, who, by grace and
   inspiration of the Holy Spirit,
   are poured into the hearts of the faithful
   so that from their faithless state,
   they may be made faithful servants of God
   through you.

Two Greetings of St. Francis of Assisi

*G*ood morning, good people!
Peace and all good!

Peace Prayer of St. Francis of Assisi

*L*ord, make me an instrument of your peace.
Where there is hatred, let me sow love;
 where there is injury, pardon;
 where there is doubt, faith;
 where there is despair, hope;
 where there is darkness, light;
 and where there is sadness, joy.

O divine Master, grant that I may not so
 much seek to be consoled as to console;
 to be understood as to understand;
 to be loved as to love.
For it is in giving that we receive;
 it is in pardoning that we are pardoned;
 and it is in dying that we are born to
 eternal life. Amen.

Salutation to the Virtues

*H*ail Queen Wisdom, the Lord salutes you
with your sister Holy-Pure Simplicity.
Lady Holy Poverty, the Lord salutes you
with your sister Holy Humility.
Lady Holy Charity, the Lord salutes you
with your sister Holy Obedience.

Most holy virtues, the Lord salutes all of you,
he from whom you come and proceed.
There is scarcely anyone in all the world
who can have one of you before they die.
They who have one and offend not the
　others, have all. And they who offend one,
　have none and offend all. *(cf. James 2:10)*
And any whatsoever confounds vices and sins.
Holy Wisdom confounds Satan and all his
wickedness.

Pure Holy Simplicity confounds all the
　wisdom of this world *(cf. 1 Corinthians 2:6)*
and the wisdom of the body.

Holy Poverty confounds cupidity and
　avarice and the cares of this world.
Holy Humility confounds pride and all
people who are in the world, and likewise

all the things which are in the world.

Holy Charity confounds all the diabolic and carnal temptations and all carnal fears.

Holy Obedience confounds all things corporal, both carnal and one's own willings and holds the body mortified in obedience to the spirit and in obedience to one's brother or sister and is subject and submissive to all persons who are in the world and not only to persons, but even to the beasts and the wildlife, so that they might do with him, whatever they will, as much as it will have been given them from above by the Lord *(cf. John 19:11)*.

Prayer of the Church to St. Francis

*P*raised be my Lord and God, with all his creatures, and especially our brother the sun, who brings us the day and brings us the light; fair is he, and he shines with great splendor.

O Lord, he is a sign to us of you!
Praised be my Lord for our sister the moon,
and for the stars, set clear and lovely in the heaven.

Immaculate Conception Novena Prayer of St. Francis of Assisi

*H*ail, holy Lady,
   Most holy Queen,
Mary, Mother of God,
Virgin made Church;
Chosen by the most holy Father in heaven,
consecrated by him,
with his most holy beloved Son
and the Holy Spirit, the Comforter.
On you descended and in you still remains
all the fullness of grace
and every good.

Hail, his Palace,
   his Tabernacle.
Hail, his Robe.
Hail, his handmaid.
Hail, his Mother.
And hail, all holy virtues
   who, by the grace
   and inspiration of the Holy Spirit,
   are poured forth into the hearts of the faithful
so that, faithless no longer,
they may be made faithful servants of God
   through you. Amen.

Prayer of St. Francis
Inspired by the Lord's Prayer

*O*ur Father
Our Creator, Redeemer,
Comforter and Savior.

Who art in heaven.
You are with the angels and the saints,
bathing them in your light that they may
be enlightened by your love, and
dwelling within them that they may be

filled with your joy. You are the supreme good, the eternal good, from whom comes all goodness, and without whom there is no goodness.

Hallowed be your name.
May our knowledge of you become ever clearer, that we may know the breadth of your blessings, the length of your promises, the height of your majesty, and the depth of your judgments.

Your kingdom come.
Rule in our hearts with your grace, that we may become fit subjects for your kingdom. We desire nothing more than to dwell in your kingdom, where we can watch you on your throne, and enjoy your perfect love.

Your will be done, on earth as it is in heaven.
May we love you with our whole heart by always thinking of you, with our whole soul by always desiring you, with our whole mind by directing all our intentions to you, and with our whole

strength by spending all our energies in your service. And may we love our neighbors as ourselves, drawing them to your love, rejoicing in their good fortunes, and caring for them in their misfortunes.

Give us this day our daily bread.
In memory and understanding and reverence of the love which our Lord Jesus Christ has for us, revealed by his sacrifice for us on the cross, we ask for the perfect bread of his body.

And forgive us our trespasses.
We know that you forgive us, through the suffering and death of your beloved Son.

As we forgive those who trespass against us.
Enable us to forgive perfectly and without reserve any wrong that has been committed against us. And strengthen our hearts truly to love our enemies, praying for them and striving to serve them.

And lead us not into temptation.
Save us not only from obvious and persistent temptations, but also those that are hidden or come suddenly when our guard is lowered.

But deliver us from evil.
Protect us from past evil, protect us against present evil, and free us from future evil.

Prayers to St. Francis

Prayer for Animals

God our heavenly Father, you created the world to serve humanity's needs and to lead them to you. By our own fault we have lost the beautiful relationship which we once had with all your creation. Help us to see that by restoring our relationship with you we will also restore it with all your creation. Give us the grace to see all animals as gifts from you and to treat them with respect for they are your creation. We pray for all the animals who are suffering as a result of our neglect. May the order you originally established be once again restored to the whole world through the intercession of the glorious Virgin Mary, the prayers of St. Francis and the merits of your Son, our Lord Jesus Christ who lives and reigns with you now and forever. Amen.

Blessing for All Animals

*B*lessed are you, Lord God,
Maker of all living creatures.
On the fifth and sixth days of creation
 you called forth fish in the sea,
 birds in the air and animals on the land.
You inspired St. Francis to call all animals
 his brothers and sisters.
We ask you to bless this animal.
By the power of your love
 enable it to live according to your plan.
May we always praise you
 for all your beauty in creation.
Blessed are you, Lord our God, in all your
creatures! Amen.

Blessing for a Sick Animal

*H*eavenly Father,
 you created all things for your glory
 and made us stewards of this creature.
If it is your will, restore it to health and
 strength.
Blessed are you, Lord God, and holy is your
 name forever and ever. Amen.

Prayer for the Feast of St. Francis of Assisi

O God who, through the merits of blessed Francis, magnifies your Church, enriching it anew with spiritual offering: make us, like him, to disdain the goods of earth, nor at any time to lack the comforting gifts of heaven.

(From the Roman Missal)

St. Francis of Assisi, help us. By your example may we learn that life does not consist in the pursuit of wealth nor in the abundance of our possessions.

St. Francis of Assisi, come to our aid. Because we live at a time when people glorify ease and seek after luxuries, and when many wish only the gratification of fleshly desires, we stand in special need of your singleminded dedication to Christ in the narrow way that leads to life.

St. Francis of Assisi, assist us now. May we appreciate as you did the beauties of God's wonderful creation, and the glory of the world he made for us. Help us to enjoy and appreciate

God's bounty without spoiling or defacing his gifts by our heedlessness and greed.

Teach us, seraphic Father Francis, to value all things as Christ did and to be imitators of him as you were. May we thus enjoy the good things of life, but always prefer the blessings of the endless life to come. Amen.

St. Francis, the little poor man of Assisi, we invoke you as the admirable mirror you were of our divine Master.

You imitated Christ the Lord in your humility and obedience. You faithfully followed him in poverty and weakness. With joy you accepted suffering, contempt, and trials for the sake of his name.

In your goodness help us, then, to imitate your example. By your power with God obtain for us the special favor we now seek through your intercession.

Please pray for us, gentle and happy saint of the poor, that we may always be loyal followers of our Savior, Jesus Christ, and filled always with divine riches. Amen.

Novena to St. Francis of Assisi

Glorious St. Francis, who voluntarily renounced all the comforts and riches of your home to follow more perfectly the life of poverty and self-denial of Jesus Christ:

> obtain for us, we pray, a generous contempt of all things in this world, that we may secure the true and eternal things of heaven.

Glory by to the Father, and to the Son, and to the Holy Spirit. Amen.

O glorious St. Francis, who during the whole course of your life continually wept over the passion of the Redeemer, and labor most zealously for the salvation of souls:

> obtain for us, we pray, the grace of weeping continually over those sins by which we have crucified afresh our

> Lord Jesus Christ, that we may attain to be of the number of those who shall eternally bless his supreme mercy.

Glory by to the Father, and to the Son, and to the Holy Spirit. Amen.

O glorious St. Francis who, loving above all things suffering and the cross, merited to bear in your body the miraculous stigmata, by which you became a living image of Jesus Christ crucified:

> obtain for us, we pray, the grace to bear in our bodies the mortification of Christ, that we may merit one day to receive the consolations which are infallibly promised to all those who now weep.

"If we be dead with Jesus Christ, we shall live also with him," says the apostle; "if we suffer, we shall also reign with him."
(2 Timothy 2:11-12).

Pray for us, St. Francis, that we may obtain the

graces and favors we ask in this novena; pray for us, especially, that we may obtain the grace of perseverance; of a holy death and a happy eternity.

Our Father, Hail Mary, Glory Be *(repeated five times each)*.